Startup Funding Mastery:

Proven strategies for success

Steps to fuel your start-up's journey with over $200,000 in grants & services, no matter your growth stage.

by

Chuka Okeke

Co-founder Musha

Copyright © 2024 by Chuka Okeke

All rights reserved. No part of this publication may be reproduced, distributed, or transmitted in any form or by any means, including photocopying, recording, or other electronic or mechanical methods, without the prior written permission of the publisher, except in the case of brief quotations embodied in critical reviews and certain other non-commercial uses permitted by copyright law. For permission requests, write to the publisher at the address below.

Publisher: Chuka Okeke

Contact Information: Startupfaundri@gmail.com

Disclaimer: The information in this eBook is provided "as is" without any representations or warranties, express or implied. The author makes no representations or warranties in relation to the information in this eBook.

First Edition.

Contents

Module 1: Introduction 4
    Lesson 1.1: Overview of Microsoft Founders Hub [1] 4
    Lesson 1.2: Eligibility and Application Process 9

Module 2: Preparing Your Start-up for Funding 20
    Lesson 2.1: Building a Strong Business Plan 20
    Lesson 2.2: Crafting a Compelling Pitch 24

Module 3: Leveraging Microsoft Resources 27
    Lesson 3.1: Utilizing Azure Credits and Tools 27
    Lesson 3.2: Accessing Expert Guidance 33
    Lesson 3.3: Maximizing the value of mentorship 38

Module 4: Networking and Community Building 39
    Lesson 4.1: Expanding Your Network 39
    Lesson 4.2: Building a Supportive Community 45

Module 5: Final Project and Course Wrap-Up 48
    Lesson 5.1: Developing Your Funding Strategy 48
    Lesson 5.2: Presenting your strategy for feedback & optimization 54
    Lesson 5.3: Course Summary and Next Steps 57

Additional Resources 62
    List of recommended reading and online resources 62

Module 1: Introduction

Lesson 1.1: Overview of Microsoft Founders Hub

The big question would be, *"What is the Microsoft Founders Hub?"* Have you heard of it? Have you seen it anywhere as you spend time online on social media or other online platforms? Let's get right into it.

Microsoft Founders Hub is a program designed to support start-ups and early-stage companies in their growth and innovation journey. The program aims to foster collaboration and knowledge sharing between Microsoft and start-up founders, providing a platform for mutual learning and growth.

The program empowers start-ups to build and scale their businesses, leveraging Microsoft's expertise, resources, and network. It offers a tailored experience for founders, providing access to Microsoft's ecosystem, including its technical expertise, industry connections, and market opportunities.

Microsoft Founders Hub is particularly interested in start-ups working on innovative solutions in areas like artificial intelligence, machine learning, cloud computing, and more. By joining the program, start-ups can tap into Microsoft's extensive resources and expertise, gaining valuable insights and support to drive their success.

The program is designed to be flexible and adaptive, recognizing the unique needs and challenges of each start-up. By providing a supportive and collaborative environment, Microsoft Founders Hub aims to help start-ups achieve their full potential and make a meaningful impact in their respective industries.

Benefits of joining the program

The Microsoft Founders Hub offers a plethora of benefits worth well over $200,000 and this is why it is one of the most sought-after programs out there. The following benefits stand out [1][2][3];

- Free access to leading AI models, including OpenAI GPT-4, to accelerate innovation.

- Up to $150k in Azure credits, GitHub, Microsoft 365, LinkedIn Premium, and more to ship products faster. This includes services with their other partners like Stripe Mira etc. to help you and your start-up with different aspects of your processes.

- Unlimited 1:1 meetings with Microsoft experts across various specialties to unblock barriers and receive guidance.

- Technical advisory and consulting services, including 1:1 technical advisory with expert engineers on the platform.

- Access to a global team of experts and mentors for guidance on topics like scaling, go-to-market strategy, and fundraising.

- Up to $150,000 in credits to access leading AI models through Azure.

- Experimentation with large language models for free with $2,500 in OpenAI credits.

- Free access to GitHub Enterprise, VS Code, Azure OpenAI Service, and more.

- Start-up-friendly offers from trusted partners like Bubble, sales and marketing platforms, LinkedIn Premium, and more.

- Free access to Microsoft tools and platforms like Azure AI services, Microsoft 365, and more.

- Integration with development tools like GitHub, VS Code, and more.

- Enterprise-grade security and compliance features.

- Access to Microsoft Power Platform, Dynamics 365, and Visual Studio Enterprise.

- Expert Network, with a carefully curated team of experts for one-on-one guidance.

- Self-guided learning and personalized training content for founders.

- Pairing with an Azure engineer for technical advisory sessions.

Success stories and case studies

Seeing is believing as they say. It will interest you to know that the following notable start-ups including my company, have all gone through this program and have gained immensely through it. Here are some success stories and case studies from the Microsoft Founders Hub program [4]:

1. **Duhqa:** Long-term support and benefits were key to Duhqa's success. They gained a path for listing their application in the Microsoft Commercial Marketplace, providing access to a vast customer base.

2. **Tuniverse:** Azure credits allowed Tuniverse to build and maintain development and production environments without high costs, enabling it to focus on growth and innovation.

3. **PubHive:** Key technology insights and help passing industry audits were instrumental to PubHive's success. Their AI-powered SaaS platform benefited from Microsoft's expertise, ensuring compliance and scalability.

4. **Olaris:** Having a Microsoft stamp of approval has been invaluable to this woman-led start-up. Olaris gained credibility and visibility, attracting customers and partners with the backing of a trusted technology leader.

Others include;

- **PORGiESOFT:** They were able to deploy and host their anti-fraud SMS-phishing solution via Azure's App Service.

- **Bumpy:** Free access to Microsoft software and technology was huge for this small start-up.

- **Adless:** Azure credits helped offset costs and preserve the runway for their bootstrapped company.

- **HAAT Delivery:** The program helped them work more efficiently and grow much faster than they would have otherwise.

Lesson 1.2: Eligibility and Application Process

The big question is, *Who can apply?*

The Microsoft for Start-ups Founders Hub is open to all individuals, from students with innovative ideas to seasoned founders[1]. The main eligibility requirements for Microsoft for Start-ups Founders Hub are as follows [1]:

- Start-ups must be building a software-based product or service.

- Must be privately held and for-profit entities to be eligible.

- Has not received Series D or later funding.

- Has previously received less than $10,000 in Azure credits.

Step-by-step guide to the application process

The application process is quite straightforward if you understand the process and abide by the rules. To apply, you would need to have a LinkedIn account [1] and a working device with good internet access. You can apply through the official website [1].

Before applying for the Microsoft Founders Hub, which I will lay down the process below, you need to do the following;

- Review the eligibility criteria and program benefits as stated at the beginning of this section.
- Fill out the online application form, providing detailed information about your start-up, including your pitch, product, market, and team.
- Upload required documents, such as your business plan and pitch deck. Depending on the level you are applying for, you might not need to submit these documents until you are ready to apply for later stages.
- After you have done the above, submit your application and wait for review. If selected, you'll receive an invitation to join the program. This would typically take 2-4 days for the decision to get back to you.
- Upon successful enrolment, complete the onboarding process, including setting up your Azure account and accessing resources. Finally, leverage the program's benefits, including mentorship, networking opportunities, and technical support, to accelerate your start-up's growth."

The steps and recommendations for filling out the application form have been outlined below.

1. Navigate to the Program's application portal using this link: *https://foundershub.startups.microsoft.com/signup*

   Here, click on the 'Apply with LinkedIn' button which takes you through the automatic authentication process and loads up the application form.

   NB: If you do not have a LinkedIn account as mentioned previously you cannot get past this stage.

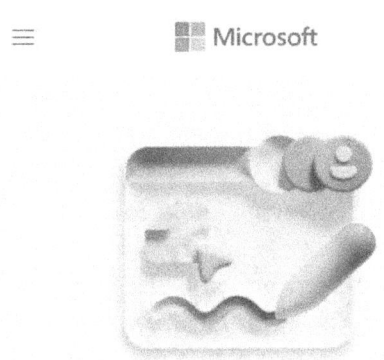

Accelerate your startup growth with AI

Microsoft for Startups Founders Hub provides free access to leading AI models through Azure, including OpenAI GPT-4, up to $150,000 in Azure credits, one-on-one guidance from Microsoft experts, and so much more. Open to anyone with an idea—no funding required.

Apply with LinkedIn

2. After authenticating your LinkedIn account, your basic details would have already been taken. You can then select your gender and talk about yourself and why you are best suited to lead the company.

   NB: It's always good to link a personal experience or expertise you possess to the start-up you are applying for.

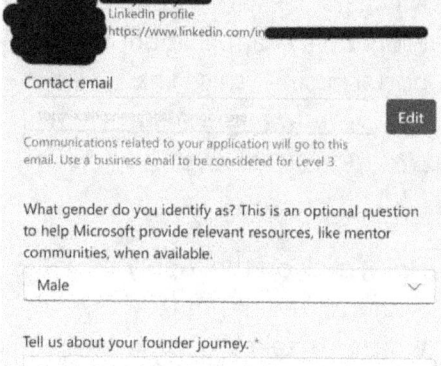

3. In this step you have to add the details of your start-up, some of the fields are already populated so you just select what applies to you. Just ensure to fill in all mandatory fields.

Your start-up idea can be your college project that you are building into a software/technology-focused company.

2. Explain your startup or idea

It's never too early to get started with us. If you're ideating, we just need a working name for your project and a description of your solution. The more you share, the better we'll understand your vision.

Startup or project name *

> The name of your solution

Startup or project website

> Your company URL if you have one

Provide a description of your software solution *

> Include your value proposition, target market, and product differentiation

What is your primary business model? *

What industry does your startup or project serve? *

What categories most closely describe your product? Choose all that apply

Share a product demo or idea overview video.

> Your video link via YouTube, Vimeo, or other platform

Must be a publicly available link (not password-protected or private drive)

foundershub.startups.microsoft.com — Private

4. At this point, you select the stage of your company and the funding you have received if any. You also have to select the type of founder you are (technical or non-technical).

Here, Technical refers to founders who code or are involved in other technical aspects of developing the product while Non-technical simply refers to a founder who is not involved in the technical aspect of the product development.

3. Provide us with a few more details

Every business grows at a different pace. Help us understand where you are right now in your journey.

What development stage best describes your startup or project? *

How to pick your stage.

What is the funding stage associated with your startup or project? *

How would you describe yourself as a founder? *

5. As a continuation of the 3rd section, you will have to declare the level of experience you have with Azure (you have to choose between Expert, Moderate, and Novice), any Microsoft or other partners you are already working with, and also if your start-up is focused on social impact for which I would leave as "No" as they are more interested in for-profit companies.

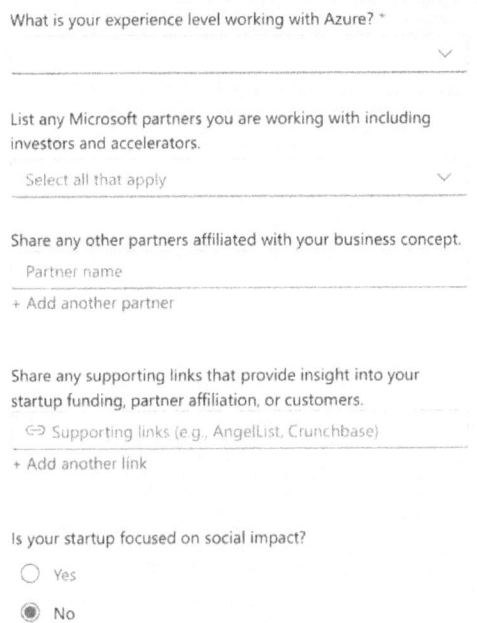

6. In the final section, you have to add the registered/trading address of the company if incorporated or your home address if you have yet to register the company.

   After the form has been filled, Click on submit and await a confirmation email acknowledging the receipt of your application.

Common pitfalls and how to avoid them

We do know things can go wrong and with the experience we have curated, we can confidently say these are the most common pitfalls to avoid when applying and how to overcome them.

1. Lack of clarity: You have to clearly articulate your start-up's mission, vision, product, and goals. This helps in showing you have a basic understanding of the business concept you are looking to venture into.

2. Insufficient information: Provide detailed information about your start-up, including your team, market, and competitive landscape. You can also add a little about your competition and how you are better here.

3. Unrealistic expectations: Be realistic about what the program can offer and what you hope to achieve with what is on offer.

4. Poor fit: Ensure your start-up aligns with Microsoft's focus areas and technologies as it helps increase your chances of being selected for the program.

5. Inadequate preparation: Prepare a solid pitch, demo, or prototype to showcase your start-up's potential. This will help with the later stages but is not necessary for the earlier stages of the funding process.

6. Neglecting to showcase traction: Highlight any progress, milestones, or user acquisition achievements.

7. Inability to scale: Demonstrate a clear plan for scaling your business. If this is not clear at the moment you can talk about potential partnerships which can help you scale or expand your market share. You can always modify this later on if you are still applying for the earlier stages.

8. Ignoring program requirements: Carefully review and make sure you meet the program's eligibility criteria and application requirements.

9. Lack of responsiveness: Respond promptly to inquiries and requests from the Microsoft for Start-ups team. Sometimes your application may need a bit more information and this can lead to your application being sent back to you for further review.

10. Unwillingness to engage: Actively participate in program offerings, mentorship, and

networking opportunities as this helps you make the most out of the program

By avoiding these common pitfalls, you can increase your chances of a successful application and maximize the benefits of the Microsoft for Start-ups Founders Hub program.

Refer to the additional resources section towards the end of the page to get links for further reading and resources to learn more [1][2][3][4][5].

Module 2: Preparing Your Start-up for Funding

You now know about the programme, its advantages, how to act positively, and what to avoid doing in order to succeed. This part will cover preparing your start-up for funding as well as the steps you need to take to prepare the necessary paperwork for the Microsoft Founders Hub programme and other start-up initiatives that call for it.

Lesson 2.1: Building a Strong Business Plan

For your start-up to thrive and to get finance, you need a solid business plan. It outlines your company's objectives, tactics, and financial projections and acts as a roadmap. A well-written business plan aids in maintaining focus and drawing in investors by outlining your operational and financial plans, describing your mission clearly, and doing a market analysis. A strong business plan is an essential tool for success, regardless of your stage of development or goals for expansion.

Now that we have this information, let's examine what makes a strong business strategy.

Key components of a business plan

1. **Executive Summary**: A brief overview of your business, including your mission statement, product/service offerings, and basic information about your leadership team, employees, and location.
2. **Company Description**: Detailed information about your business, including the problems it solves, the market needs it addresses, and your business structure.
3. **Market Analysis**: Research on your industry, market size, expected growth, and your target market.
4. **Organization and Management**: Your business's organizational structure, details about the ownership, and profiles of your management team.
5. **Products or Services**: Information about what you're selling or your services, including the benefits to your customers.
6. **Marketing and Sales Strategy**: How you plan to attract and retain customers, and your sales strategy.
7. **Funding Request**: If you're seeking funding, outline your funding requirements, potential

future funding requirements over the next five years, and how you plan to use the funds.
8. **Financial Projections**: Provide financial forecasts to support your funding request, including income statements, cash flow statements, and balance sheets.

Further Reading: Refer to the additional resources section towards the end of this book to get links for further reading and resources to help you create your business plan [6].

How to Articulate Your Vision and Mission

- **Vision Statement**: Describe your long-term goals and the impact you want your business to have. Make it inspiring and aspirational. For example, "To be the leading provider of eco-friendly products that improve everyday life."

  You can also include a geographical area here. For Example; "To be the leading provider of eco-friendly products that improve everyday life in Europe". This helps show the spread of influence you aspire for.

- **Mission Statement**: Define your business's purpose and primary objectives. It should be concise and clear, explaining what you do, who you do it for, and how you do it.

For example, "To provide high-quality, sustainable products that enhance the lives of our customers while protecting the environment."

- **Communicate Effectively**: Make your vision and mission relatable by using narrative. Talk about your passion and the path that brought your business to fruition. Encouraging your audience to feel like they are a part of your project is the major goal here. You'll be nearly unstoppable once you can establish a deeper connection with your audience 7. This also holds true for your internal employees. The external resources section now includes a resource that goes into further detail on this[8].

Financial Projections and Budgeting

- **Financial Projections**: Estimate your future revenue, expenses, and profitability. This typically includes:
    - **Income Statement**: Projects your revenue, costs, and profits over a specific period.
    - **Cash Flow Statement**: Forecasts the cash inflows and outflows, helping you manage liquidity.
    - **Balance Sheet**: Provides a snapshot of your business's financial position at a specific point in time.

- **Budgeting**: Plan how you will allocate your resources to achieve your business goals. This involves:
  - **Setting Financial Goals**: Define what you want to achieve financially.
  - **Estimating Revenues and Expenses**: Predict your income and costs based on historical data and market research.
  - **Monitoring and Adjusting**: Regularly compare your actual financial performance against your budget and make necessary adjustments [9]. To help you further with this, a link to a free online resource for budgeting templates has been added to the external resource section [10].

Further Reading: Refer to the additional resources section towards the end of the page to get links for further reading and resources to help you create your business plan [11,12].

Lesson 2.2: Crafting a Compelling Pitch

Crafting a Winning Pitch: Essential Elements and Tips

A successful pitch when done right can open many doors for a start-up and is crucial to your start-up securing funding, partners, and customers. To craft a winning pitch, focus on the following essential elements:

- **Elements of a Successful Pitch**
    - Clear Value Proposition: Clearly define your unique selling point and its benefits.
    - Compelling Story: Share your vision, mission, and journey.
    - Market Opportunity: Highlight the target market and potential growth.
    - Competitive Advantage: Showcase your innovative solution.
    - Traction and Progress: Share achievements and milestones.

- **Tips for Creating an Engaging Pitch Deck**
    - Keep it Simple and Concise: Use simple language and avoid jargon.
    - Visuals Matter: Use high-quality images, charts, and graphs.
    - Focus on Key Messages: Avoid clutter and emphasize key points.
    - Practice Your Delivery: Rehearse your pitch to ensure confidence and clarity.

- **Practice Sessions and Feedback**
    - Seek Feedback: Ask mentors, peers, and potential customers for feedback.

- o Practice with Different Audiences: Tailor your pitch to various audiences.
- o Refine and Iterate: Continuously improve your pitch based on feedback.

You'll be well on your way to crafting an engaging pitch that connects with your audience by implementing these components and pointers into your presentation.

I will also be publishing a detailed course on how to develop an appropriate pitch deck relevant to the organization it is intended for, as a one-size-fits-all approach does not apply here. I will be exposing all the failures I have encountered and also insider tips I have garnered from my time being part of different start-up organizations like OneDay, Techstars, and the like.

Use this link to express your interest so you can be notified once this is ready.

https://forms.gle/MC3XXQregonUtAPy7

Module 3: Leveraging Microsoft Resources

Lesson 3.1: Utilizing Azure Credits and Tools

So far so good, *Right?* You have now learned about the program and how to apply in detail, we have now also taught you how to develop a business and financial plan for your business as you will need it in your start-up journey.

In this section, we will explore the Azure credits structure offered on the program, and the Azure platform and gain some insight into it in general and how to use it:

Structure of Azure Credits:

- Up to $150,000 in credits, available in four years at $1,000, $5,000, $25,000, and $150,000 increments.

- Tailored credit offers that grow with your business

- Every award level has a one-year duration, after which you must fulfil the requirements for the subsequent level in order to obtain further credits.

Benefits:

- Build products in the cloud

- Accelerate finding product-market fit by implementing technologies available on the hub's portal.

- Access to GitHub Enterprise, VS Code, Azure OpenAI Service, and more

- Free 24/7 Azure Standard Support

Usage:

- Build and deploy applications on Azure.

- Use credits for Azure services like computing, storage, and networking.

- Access industry-leading AI models like OpenAI GPT-4.

- Integrate with development tools like GitHub and VS Code.

External Applications:

- Use Azure credits with partner offers like Bubble, Ansarada, Datadog, and more

- Helps you access start-up-friendly offers from trusted partners on the hub like Mira, OpenAI, and more.

- Combine Azure credits with other benefits like Microsoft 365 and LinkedIn products e.g. LinkedIn Premium

Best Practices:

- Before or after going live, you can utilise credits to test new ideas and innovate on your start-up.

- Use Azure credits to fund pilots and proof-of-concepts.

- Benefit from professional advice and instructional materials on how to use your credit stash most effectively.

NB: Azure credits are redeemable over time, and their usage should align with the terms and conditions of the Microsoft for Start-ups Founders Hub program.

Essential tools and technologies available on the Azure platform

Here are some of the essential tools and technologies available on the Azure platform. More resources with an in-depth look into this are linked below [13] [14]:

- AI + machine learning: Create next-gen apps with AI capabilities

- Analytics: Store, process, analyze and visualize data

- Compute: Access cloud compute capacity and scale on demand

- Containers: Develop and manage containerized apps

- Databases: Get secure, enterprise-grade, fully managed database services

- Developer tools: Build, manage, and deliver cloud apps

- Hybrid + multi-cloud: Bring cloud innovation to on-premises workloads

- Identity: Manage user identities and access

- Integration: Integrate on-premises and cloud-based apps, data, and processes

- Internet of Things: Connect assets, discover insights, and drive actions

- Management and governance: Simplify, automate, and optimize cloud resources

- Migration: Accelerate migration to the cloud

- Mixed reality: Create immersive experiences

- Networking: Connect cloud and on-premises infrastructure

- Virtual desktop infrastructure: Empower secure remote work

- Azure Operator Insights: Deliver analytical and business insights

- Azure Operator Service Manager: Simplify operator service management

- Azure Operator Nexus: Support mission-critical mobile network apps

- Azure Programmable Connectivity: Simplify network API management

- Microsoft Azure Data Manager: Integrate data from disparate sources

- Azure SQL: Get serverless relational databases

- Azure Cosmos DB: Get a fully managed, globally distributed database service

- Azure Kubernetes Service (AKS): Get fully managed container orchestration

Case studies of successful implementations

Now that you know a little bit more, you can better understand the Azure platform and the wide range of tools that start-ups use to improve the security and productivity of their operations. The four most noteworthy start-up case studies for Azure implementation are as follows:

- WD-40: WD-40 was able to reduce expenses and boost productivity by relocating their data centre to Azure. By providing WD-40 with real-time data insights and analytics, Azure helped the organisation enhance its business operations and make better decisions.

- Florida Fish and Wildlife: By successfully migrating its data and apps to Azure, the Florida Fish and Wildlife Conservation Commission was able to increase security, save expenses, and improve efficiency.

- Team Venti: This managed service provider leverages Azure to serve its clientele with dependable and secure IT management services. Team Venti can provide scalable and adaptable IT solutions to its clients by utilising Azure.

- Creative Security: Providing cloud-based security solutions to its clientele, Creative Security, a managed security services provider, leverages Azure. Creative Security can provide its clients with cutting-edge threat detection and response capabilities thanks to Azure.

Lesson 3.2: Accessing Expert Guidance

In this section, We will be talking about how to book 1:1 meetings with Microsoft experts who can help you leverage many topics concerning your start-up's ecosystem.

To book 1:1 meetings with Microsoft experts on the Founders Hub platform, follow these steps:

1. Sign in: Log in to your Founders Hub account.

2. Navigate: Go to the "Expert Connect" or "Office Hours" section.

3. Filter: Select "Microsoft" as the expert type and choose your preferred expertise area (e.g., Azure, AI, etc.).

4. Choose an expert: Select the Microsoft expert you'd like to meet with.

5. Check availability: View the expert's available time slots.

6. Schedule: Book a meeting by selecting a time slot that suits you.

7. Add details: Provide a brief description of what you'd like to discuss during the meeting.

8. Confirm: Receive a confirmation email with the meeting details.

NB: Ensure you have a valid Founders Hub account and follow any additional instructions provided on the platform.

Topics to discuss with mentors and advisors

We hope that by now you can book sessions and even teach others how to do this. You now need to know which start-up topics are available to book a mentor for.

The topics available to be discussed with Microsoft experts on the Founders Hub platform include:

1. Azure:

   - Cloud migration and deployment

   - Architecture and design

   - Security and Compliance

   - Cost optimization

2. Artificial Intelligence (AI) and Machine Learning (ML):

   - AI/ML strategy and implementation

   - Natural Language Processing (NLP)

   - Computer Vision

   - Predictive analytics

3. Microsoft 365:

   - Microsoft Teams and Collaboration

   - SharePoint and content management

   - Office 365 and productivity

- Security and Compliance

4. Dynamics 365:

    - ERP and CRM implementation

    - Business process automation

    - Sales and marketing optimization

    - Customer service and support

5. Microsoft Graph and APIs:

    - Integration with Microsoft services

    - API development and management

    - Data analytics and visualization

6. Gaming:

    - Xbox and PC gaming development

    - Game studio operations and management

    - Gaming community engagement

7. Mixed Reality (MR) and Virtual Reality (VR):

- MR/VR development and implementation

- Immersive experiences and solutions

8. Business and Strategic Growth:

    - Business model innovation

    - Go-to-market strategy

    - Scaling and growth strategy

9. Technology and Innovation:

    - Emerging tech trends and insights

    - Innovation strategy and implementation

    - Digital transformation and modernization

NB; These topics may be subject to change, and experts may have specific areas of focus within these categories.

Lesson 3.3: Maximizing the value of mentorship

You may not be thinking about this but you should. Have you asked yourself, *How do I make these sessions efficient?* Let's take a closer look at this.

Founders like you should approach mentorship with defined goals and an open mind to get the most out of it at the Microsoft Founders Hub. To get advice and criticism, you should actively look for mentors who have the necessary training and experience. You should also schedule frequent check-ins with them. Along with these, you should be ready to share your goals and advancement, pose meaningful questions, and be open to receiving helpful criticism. By doing this, you can use mentoring to overcome obstacles, obtain insightful knowledge, and quicken the growth of your start-up. Furthermore, entrepreneurs such as yourself ought to be prepared to give back by serving as mentors to others, fostering a climate of information exchange and community development in the Microsoft Founders Hub and other communities, all of which contribute to your improvement.

Module 4: Networking and Community Building

Lesson 4.1: Expanding Your Network

Importance of networking for start-ups

Have you ever thought, *How do I leverage networking for my start-up?* Before we talk more on that, you have to know that networking is crucial for start-ups as it offers numerous benefits, including but not limited to:

> 1. Access to resources: When you connect with potential/relevant investors, mentors, and partners you are bound to have access to resources to aid you on your journey.
>
> 2. Collaboration and partnerships: Find opportunities for joint ventures, supplier relationships, and strategic alliances. This can only happen easily if you network the right way.

3. Talent acquisition: Meet potential employees, advisors, or board members. This can be through events, forums, and even the most unlikely places.

4. Market feedback: Gain insights from potential customers, industry experts, and peers. Very important and can be a great tool for improvement if you connect deeply with your market.

5. Visibility and branding: Increase your start-up's profile and establish thought leadership.

6. Support system: Build relationships with fellow entrepreneurs, mentors, and industry experts for guidance and encouragement.

7. Learning and knowledge sharing: Stay updated on industry trends, best practices, and innovative solutions.

8. Funding opportunities: Meet investors, angel networks, and venture capitalists. Also, check out online opportunities just like the Start-up Founders Hub and apply for pre-accelerators that can immensely aid your journey and lead you to better opportunities.

9. Customer acquisition: Connect with potential customers, partners, and suppliers via industry events and in-house events.

10. Strategic guidance: Receive valuable advice from experienced entrepreneurs, mentors, and industry experts.

By networking, you can accelerate your growth, reduce costs, and increase their chances of success.

Now that you are aware of the major benefits and impact of networking, we will provide you with the channels through which you can connect with other founders and potential investors.

These include;

1. Attending industry events, conferences, and meetups; This gets you in front of key decision-makers in your space and potentially you get to see other founders with who you might need to partner to improve and enhance your product's offerings.

2. Joining online communities, forums, and social media groups (e.g., LinkedIn, Twitter, Facebook).

3. Participating in start-up accelerators, incubators, and co-working spaces.

4. Leveraging networking platforms (e.g., LinkedIn, Crunchbase, AngelList).

5. Reaching out to founders and investors directly via email or message. This works better when you have been previously introduced by someone they know.

6. Joining local entrepreneurial organizations and networking groups.

7. Using event platforms like Eventbrite, Meetup, and Lanyrd to find relevant events.

8. Connecting with alumni networks from your university or previous companies.

9. Joining online mentorship platforms like MentorNet, eMentor, or MicroMentor.

10. Taking part in start-up competitions, hackathons, and pitch events.

Some popular platforms for connecting with founders and investors include but are not limited to:

- LinkedIn: https://www.linkedin.com
- Crunchbase: https://www.crunchbase.com
- AngelList: https://angel.co
- Twitter: https://twitter.com
- Founders Network: https://foundersnetwork.com (Note: This is an exclusive network, and you need to apply to join)
- Startup Grind: https://www.startupgrind.com
- Entrepreneur's Organization (EO): https://www.eonetwork.org
- YPO (Young Presidents' Organization): https://www.ypo.org *(Note: This is an exclusive network, and you need to apply to join)*
- Start-up Founders & Investors (LinkedIn group): https://www.linkedin.com/groups/1234567 (You'll need to join the group on LinkedIn)
- Founder2be: https://www.founder2be.com

NB: *Please note that some of these platforms may require you to create an account, apply for membership, or receive an invitation to join.*

Remember, networking is about building genuine relationships and providing value to others, not just asking for favours or promoting yourself.

Participating in Microsoft Founders Hub events

Considering that this course is focused on impacting you with knowledge of the Microsoft Founders Hub, it would not be complete if we did not tell you how to attend the events organized for the program's participants. To access these events, follow these steps:

- Visit the Microsoft for Start-ups Blog to find upcoming events

- Check Eventbrite for upcoming Microsoft for Start-ups Founders Hub events

- Register for the desired event, providing the necessary details

- Mark your calendar for the event date and time

- Attend the event, engage with speakers, and network with attendees

- Leverage resources and connections made during the event

- Visit the Microsoft for Start-ups Founders Hub website for on-demand content and additional resources

- Join the Founders Hub community for access to future events and exclusive benefits

Refer to the additional resources section towards the end of the page to get links for further reading and resources to help you access these events [15][16].

Lesson 4.2: Building a Supportive Community

In this section, we will be talking about creating a community around your start-up. After all, with all the networking going on, there has to be other actions that help in positioning your company perfectly in the public eye. Now you might be asking, *How do I get this done?*

Building a community around your start-up can be a game-changer for your business. Here are some key steps to help you get started:

1. **Define Your Mission and Values**: Clearly articulate the problem your start-up is solving and the values that drive your business. This will attract like-minded individuals who share your vision.
2. **Start Small and Personal**: Begin by engaging with a few early adopters. Make them feel special and valued. Personal interactions can help build strong, loyal relationships.
3. **Create Valuable Content**: Share content that resonates with your community. This could be blog posts, videos, webinars, or social media

updates. The goal is to provide value and keep your community engaged.
4. **Leverage Social Media and Online Platforms**: Use social media to connect with your audience. Platforms like Facebook, LinkedIn, and Twitter can help you reach a wider audience and foster engagement.
5. **Host Events and Meetups**: Organize events, both online and offline, to bring your community together. This can help strengthen relationships and create a sense of belonging.
6. **Encourage Participation and Feedback**: Make your community feel heard by encouraging them to share their thoughts and feedback. This can help you improve your product and make your community feel more invested in your success.
7. **Recognize and Reward Members**: Show appreciation for your community members by recognizing their contributions and offering rewards. This can help build loyalty and encourage more active participation.
8. **Be Consistent and Authentic**: Consistency in your communication and actions builds trust. Be genuine and transparent with your community to foster a strong, lasting relationship.

Building a community takes time and effort, but the benefits of having a loyal and engaged group of supporters can be invaluable for your start-up's growth and success. Do you have any specific goals or challenges in mind for your community-building efforts?

Further Reading: Refer to the additional resources section towards the end of the page to get links for further reading and resources to help you learn more on how to build and manage a community around your start-up [15][16].

Module 5: Final Project and Course Wrap-Up

Lesson 5.1: Developing Your Funding Strategy

Finally, in this last section, we are taking you back to the beginning. Creating a personalized funding strategy for your start-up is one of the major things you must do to make decisions around funding. It even helps to know if applying to the Microsoft Founders' Hub Program suits your company's strategy for funding.

With this knowledge, you can channel your energy towards the right networking events and partners to avoid wasting your and their time. The question you might be asking is, *How do I get this sorted out?* Creating a personalized funding strategy for your start-up involves several key steps. Here's a detailed guide to help you through the process:

1. Define Your Funding Needs

- **Assess Your Financial Requirements**: Determine how much capital you need to achieve your next milestones. For this, you should already have a road map outlining your milestones and when you intend to accomplish them. This includes but is not limited to operational costs, marketing expenses, product development, and any other critical expenditures.

- **Set Clear Goals**: Identify what you aim to achieve with the funds. This could be reaching a certain revenue target, expanding your team, launching a new product or feature, etc.

2. Understand Your Funding Options

Understanding your business strategy is essential before pursuing finance as it guides your funding strategy. When choosing which funding possibilities to investigate, it could be easy to make mistakes if there is no obvious correlation between these two. Certain finance sources suit different types of enterprises better than others. Some of the funding options have been outlined and briefly explained below;

- **Bootstrapping:** Financing activities with personal savings or money made by the company.

- **Friends and Family:** Obtaining financial support from individuals close to you who share your vision.
- **Angel Investors:** High-net-worth individuals who offer capital in exchange for convertible debt or equity are known as angel investors.
- **Venture Capital:** Investing in start-ups with significant growth potential in exchange for equity.
- **Crowdfunding:** Gathering modest sums of money from a large number of individuals, usually through internet platforms.

3. Develop a Timeline

- **Plan Your Funding Rounds**: Decide when you will need to raise funds and how much you will need at each stage. This helps in avoiding cash flow issues and ensures you are prepared for each funding round.
- **Set Milestones**: Align your funding needs with specific business milestones to demonstrate progress and attract investors.

4. Create a Compelling Pitch Deck

- **Executive Summary**: Provide a brief overview of your business, including your mission, vision, and value proposition.
- **Problem and Solution**: Clearly articulate the problem your start-up is solving and how your solution addresses it.
- **Market Opportunity**: Highlight the size and growth potential of your target market.
- **Business Model**: Explain how your start-up plans to make money.
- **Traction**: Showcase any progress you have made, such as user growth, revenue, or partnerships.
- **Team**: Introduce your team and their relevant experience.
- **Financial Projections**: Provide realistic financial forecasts and key metrics.
- **Funding Ask**: Specify how much funding you are seeking and how you plan to use it.

5. Identify Potential Investors

- **Research Investors**: Look for investors who have a history of investing in your industry or stage of business. Use platforms like AngelList, Crunchbase, and LinkedIn to find potential investors.

- **Network**: Attend industry events, pitch competitions, and networking meetups to connect with investors. Leverage your existing network for introductions.

6. Approach Investors

- **Tailor Your Pitch**: Customize your pitch for each investor, highlighting aspects of your business that align with their interests and investment criteria.
- **Follow-Up**: After initial meetings, follow up with additional information and updates to keep investors engaged.

7. Negotiate Terms

- **Understand Valuation**: Be prepared to discuss your start-up's valuation and how you arrived at it. You might want to read up on how to value your start-up.
- **Term Sheets**: Familiarize yourself with common terms and conditions in investment deals, such as equity percentage, board seats, liquidation preferences, etc.
- **Seek Legal Advice**: Work with a lawyer to ensure you understand the terms and protect your interests.

8. Close the Deal

- **Due Diligence**: Be ready to provide detailed information about your business during the due diligence process.
- **Final Agreement**: Once terms are agreed upon, finalize the investment agreement and complete the necessary legal documentation.

9. Maintain Investor Relations

- **Regular Updates**: Keep your investors informed about your progress with regular updates and reports.
- **Engage Investors**: Involve your investors in strategic decisions and leverage their expertise and networks to help grow your business.

Creating a personalized funding strategy requires careful planning and execution. Following these steps can increase your chances of securing the right funding for your start-up's growth and success. *Do you have any specific questions or areas you'd like to focus on further?*

Further Reading: Refer to the additional resources section towards the end of the page to get links for further reading and resources to help you develop and optimize your funding strategy[17][18]. You can access this extra resource for templates that help you do this [19].

Lesson 5.2: Presenting the strategy for feedback & optimization

Cheers! You have now created your funding strategy and might ask, *What do I do next?* Surely, there are a couple of things you can do but the most important one is to present your strategy to the class for feedback. This could be your co-founders, mentors, and other important stakeholders in your company. To do this, you can follow these steps:

1. Prepare a clear and concise presentation (e.g., slides, handouts) summarizing your strategy.
2. Focus on key points, such as:
   - Problem statement
   - Target market
   - Unique value proposition
   - Competitive advantage
   - Business model
   - Goals and metrics

3. Practice your presentation to ensure clarity and confidence.

4. Share your presentation with the relevant stakeholders, either in person or virtually.

5. Encourage feedback and questions from your peers.

6. Actively listen to comments and suggestions, taking notes and asking clarifying questions.

7. Be open to constructive criticism and use it as an opportunity to refine your strategy.

8. Thank your peers for their input and feedback.

Some popular presentation tools you can explore, include;

1. PowerPoint

2. Google Slides

3. Keynote

4. Prezi

5. Canva

Remember to keep your presentation concise, visually engaging, and focused on the key elements of your strategy.

Final adjustments and improvements

The following last-minute tweaks and enhancements should be your team's goal before submitting a financing application:

1. Make your pitch more polished: Create a pitch that is distinct, succinct, and captivating that emphasises your market potential, competitive advantage, and unique value proposition. Don't forget to incorporate any pertinent suggestions that have previously been made.

2. Confirm the market: Make sure you are well-versed in the demands, problems, and development possibilities of your target market.

3. Fortify your group: Make sure the people on your founding team have the knowledge, experience, and abilities needed to carry out your vision.

4. Create a solid business plan: Give a clear description of your cost structure, revenue sources, and scaling strategy.

5. Make your financial forecasts more accurate: Provide accurate and thorough financial projections that take into account cash flow, expenses, and income.

6. Improve your good or service: Make sure it is unique, easy to use, and fits the demands of your intended audience.

7. Create a powerful online presence by creating a content strategy, social media presence, and expert website.

8. Create a network: Get in touch with partners, mentors, advisors, and future clients.

9. Defend your intellectual property: To protect your inventions, register trademarks, patents, and copyrights.

10. Verify adherence to laws and regulations: Acquire the required licences, authorizations, and legal records.

11. Create a thorough business plan: Describe your three to five-year plan, including your objectives and strategies.

12. Get input and make revisions: Get input from peers, mentors, and prospective clients, then make the required changes.

Lesson 5.3: Course Summary and Next Steps

Recap of key learnings

As we wind down to the final bits and bubbles, here is a recap of all the highlights contained in this course.

- We introduced you to the program and showed you its benefits, offerings, and ways to ensure you apply successfully.
- We took you through the eligibility criteria, what is required to meet the criteria, and a detailed step-by-step process of making your application and we shed light on the common mistakes and how to avoid them.
- We talked about how you can prepare your start-up for funding, and the documents and processes required.
- We walked you through how to craft a compelling pitch for your company and build a befitting pitch deck for your start-up.
- We showed you how to leverage the Microsoft resources available on the platform with a focus on Azure Credits and the mentorship platform.
- We took you through the benefits of networking for your start-up, connecting with other founders and investors, accessing the Microsoft Founders' hub events, and building a

- thriving community around your start-up.
- Finally, we walked you through the step-by-step process of creating a funding strategy for your business and provided tips on presenting it for relevant feedback from the right audience.

Next steps after completing the course

If you need extra coaching on how to go about securing the Microsoft Founders hub funding, you can schedule a 1 to 1 session with me to have a better understanding of what stage you are at and also how I can be of help.

You can schedule a free 15-minute session using the link below to get a picture of what you need to get started.

https://t.ly/vKIWS

Alternatively, you can purchase a guidance package that gives you access to multiple 1 to 1 sessions until your start-up gets accepted into the program.

Included in this package, is the review of your application documents and help in optimizing your write-ups before the submission of your application. For buying this book, you are already entitled to a 30% discount. Click on the link below to Purchase and schedule a meeting.

https://selar.co/1d0723

If you successfully secure the grant on your own, please kindly send a screenshot of the confirmation email to *startupfaundri@gmail.com*

I have aided a couple of start-ups in securing this grant funding and some of these testimonies are shared below.

Hi Chuka,

Congratulations on your acceptance to Microsoft for Startups Founders Hub! We're thrilled to welcome you on board with a mix of technical benefits and business resources including:

 $5,000 USD of Azure credits valid for one year, supported by 24/7 Azure Standard Support.

 Visual Studio Enterprise Cloud valid for the duration of your time with us.

 Personalized Azure pairing sessions for your day-to-day Azure needs and 24/7 technical support.

 Microsoft 365 valid for one year.

 Dynamics 365 valid for one year.

 $2,500 in OpenAI credits valid for 6 months.

 GitHub Enterprise Cloud valid for one year.

 PowerApps valid for one year.

Welcome to Microsoft for Startups Founders Hub

From startups-no-reply@microsoft.com
To: [redacted]
Yesterday at 17:59

Microsoft

Welcome to Microsoft for Startups Founders Hub

Hi Tony,

Congratulations on your acceptance to Microsoft for Startups Founders Hub! We're thrilled to welcome you on board with the tools and resources you need to build the future:

- Build on Azure with $1,000 USD of credits valid for one year with access to the Azure Q&A community forum for guidance and support.
- Accelerate your development with $2,500 in OpenAI credits valid for 6 months.
- Use quick-start templates in the Build with AI tab to easily deploy common generative AI solutions.

[Sign in]

To receive the above benefits and more, first review and sign your program agreement by signing in to the Microsoft for Startups Founders Hub with the LinkedIn account you used when applying.

As you develop your product and grow your business, Founders Hub grows with you. You'll be eligible for more credits at each level of your startup journey.

If you have questions, please don't hesitate to contact

Your Azure Sponsorship terms for [redacted]@gmail.com have been updated   Inbox

Microsoft Azure 7:02 pm
to me

Microsoft Azure

Your Azure Sponsorship terms have been updated

This message is to notify you that your Azure sponsorship has been updated. We're pleased to offer you free Azure usage for [redacted]@gmail.com

Usage cap: USD25000
Offer end date: August 27, 2024

If your sponsorship is still active, no action is required.

If your sponsorship is no longer active, you need to activate it to apply credit to an existing paid Azure subscription **or** to a new subscription that you create.

View your sponsorship balance and information. Use your account ID to sign in.

[Activate your sponsorship »]

Important: When activating your sponsorship, you'll be given the option to either create a new subscription, or to select the subscription you want to activate from a list of existing subscriptions. If you don't see the subscription in this list, please open a support ticket.

To apply credit to an existing subscription, first verify and/or update your credit card payment information. When submitting your request in the Azure portal:

1. For **Issue type**, select "Subscription management."
2. Select the specific subscription you want to apply credit to, and after the support plan auto-populates, select "Next."
3. For **Severity**, select "C – Minimal impact."
4. For **Problem type**, select "Switch to another offer."
5. Provide any additional details and your contact information.

Azure Support will contact you to confirm your request before activating your sponsorship and applying your credit.

Need help? Contact Azure Support

Additional Resources

List of recommended reading and online resources

1. Microsoft for Startups | Microsoft
2. Microsoft for Startups | Founders Hub benefits
3. Microsoft for Startups | Partner benefits
4. Microsoft for Startups | Founder stories
5. Medium.com | Microsoft for startups founders hub
6. Bench.co | Financial forecasting
7. Harvard Kennedy School | Articulating a vision or mission
8. CCL.org | Communicating the vision
9. Harvard Business School | Financial forecasting methods
10. Smartsheet.com | Financial projections templates
11. Founderjar.com | How to write a business plan
12. Forbes.com | How to write a business plan
13. What is Microsoft Azure and How Does It Work? (techtarget.com)
14. Directory of Azure Cloud Services | Microsoft Azure

15. Events Archives | Microsoft for Startups Blog
16. Events | Microsoft Reactor
17. Founderandlightning.com | How to create a funding strategy for your start-up
18. Fastercapital.com | Creating a Funding Strategy for Your Startup
19. Visible.vc | Startup funding proposal sample templates

Access to a community forum for ongoing support

Join our community forum where we keep tabs on people's progress and learn from the experiences of others in the start-up space. Click on the link below to declare your interest.

https://forms.gle/fj7XH6B1s53rb63FA

www.ingramcontent.com/pod-product-compliance
Lightning Source LLC
Chambersburg PA
CBHW071959210526
45479CB00003B/994